This Is to Certify That

_____ and _____

Groom   Bride

Were Joined Together in

HOLY MATRIMONY

_____ on the _____

at   day

_____ in _____

month   year

_____

By

IN THE PRESENCE OF

_____   _____

_____   _____

_____   _____

_____   _____

FAMILY

Husband's Family

_____
Father's Name

_____
Mother's Maiden Name

_____
Date of Birth

_____
Date of Birth

_____
Date of Death

_____
Date of Death

PATERNAL GRANDPARENTS

_____
Grandfather's Name

_____
Grandmother's Maiden Name

_____
Date of Birth

_____
Date of Birth

_____
Date of Death

_____
Date of Death

MATERNAL GRANDPARENTS

_____
Grandfather's Name

_____
Grandmother's Maiden Name

_____
Date of Birth

_____
Date of Birth

_____
Date of Death

_____
Date of Death

HISTORY

Wife's Family

_____

Father's Name

_____

Mother's Maiden Name

_____

Date of Birth

_____

Date of Birth

_____

Date of Death

_____

Date of Death

PATERNAL GRANDPARENTS

_____

Grandfather's Name

_____

Grandmother's Maiden Name

_____

Date of Birth

_____

Date of Birth

_____

Date of Death

_____

Date of Death

MATERNAL GRANDPARENTS

_____

Grandfather's Name

_____

Grandmother's Maiden Name

_____

Date of Birth

_____

Date of Birth

_____

Date of Death

_____

Date of Death

RECORD OF OUR CHILDREN

CHILD'S NAME

DATE OF BIRTH

PLACE OF BIRTH

MARRIED TO

DATE AND PLACE OF MARRIAGE

CHILD'S NAME

DATE OF BIRTH

PLACE OF BIRTH

MARRIED TO

DATE AND PLACE OF MARRIAGE

CHILD'S NAME

DATE OF BIRTH

PLACE OF BIRTH

MARRIED TO

DATE AND PLACE OF MARRIAGE

CHILD'S NAME

DATE OF BIRTH

PLACE OF BIRTH

MARRIED TO

DATE AND PLACE OF MARRIAGE

CHILD'S NAME

DATE OF BIRTH

PLACE OF BIRTH

MARRIED TO

DATE AND PLACE OF MARRIAGE

CHILD'S NAME

DATE OF BIRTH

PLACE OF BIRTH

MARRIED TO

DATE AND PLACE OF MARRIAGE

CHILD'S NAME

DATE OF BIRTH

PLACE OF BIRTH

MARRIED TO

DATE AND PLACE OF MARRIAGE

CHILD'S NAME

DATE OF BIRTH

PLACE OF BIRTH

MARRIED TO

DATE AND PLACE OF MARRIAGE

The Meaning
of
Marriage

Marriage was ordained by God in Eden and confirmed at the wedding in Cana of Galilee by the gracious presence and miraculous blessing of Jesus Christ. It is a sacred, unbreakable union of one man with one woman who dedicate themselves to the loving service of God, each other, their children, and their neighbor.

Marriage unites two hearts and lives, blending all their interests, sympathies and hopes. It involves mutual forebearance, loving sufferance, unwavering confidence, lifelong trust, and happiness that is found in making each other happy.

Such a solemn linking of destinies should not be effected lightly; but reverently, prayerfully, soberly, and in the fear of God. In contrast with all other earthly compacts entered into for mutual protection, advancement of interests, or hope of gain, marriage is a holy contract uniting man and woman for the establishment of a home which shall endure through all the storms and vicissitudes of life.

Whether, then, the oncoming flood of years from out the unknown future bring joy or sorrow, health or sickness, prosperity or adversity, sunshine or shadow, hopes fulfilled or dreams shattered, husband and wife are pledged to be true to each other forever, finding in reciprocated love life's greatest treasure and God's generous gift.

COME UNTO ME by Heinrich Hofmann

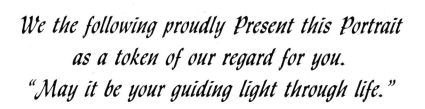

We the following proudly Present this Portrait
as a token of our regard for you.
"May it be your guiding light through life."

BELOIT SAVINGS BANK
Established 1881
Telephone 365-6645

GOODALL OIL COMPANY
Since 1905
Shell Neighborhood Stations - Fuel Oil
Telephone 365-5565

DALLMAN'S
HARDWARE - HOUSE WARES - PAINT
Telephone 362-9303

YAGLA'S
Lester Yagla - Carl Yagla - John Yagla
TV - RADIO - CAMERA HEADQUARTERS
Telephone 365-6629

DALEY - MURPHY - WISCH
FUNERAL HOME
Telephone 362-3444

FINGER PHARMACY
551 West Grand
Telephone 362-6939
DREKMIER DRUGS, INC.
443 East Grand
Telephone 364-4573

J. W. ANDERSON JEWELERS
Since 1915
Telephone 362-2352

BELOIT FLORAL CO.
Fresh Cut Flowers For All Occasions
321 State Street
Telephone 365-3353

BELOIT, WISCONSIN

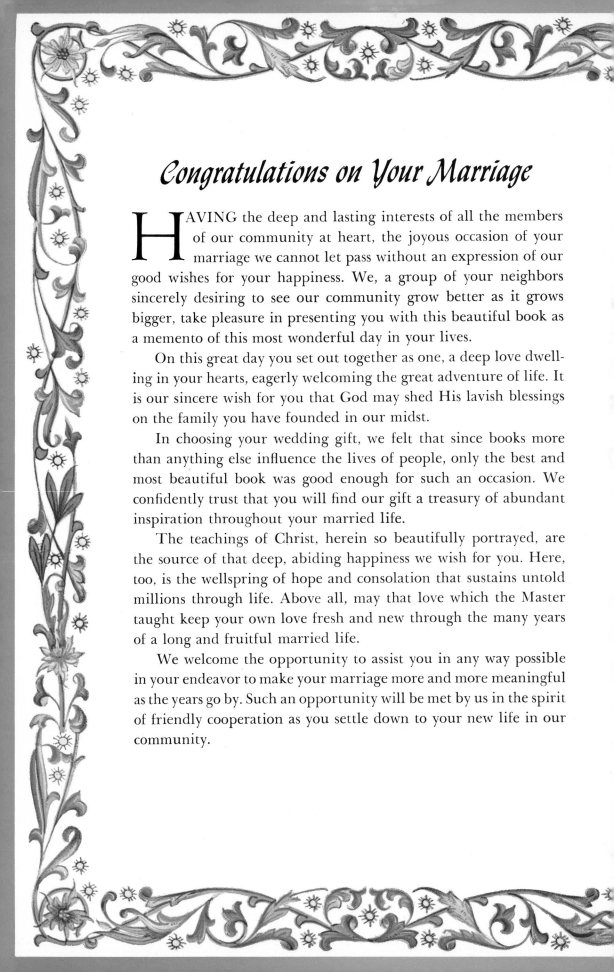

Congratulations on Your Marriage

HAVING the deep and lasting interests of all the members of our community at heart, the joyous occasion of your marriage we cannot let pass without an expression of our good wishes for your happiness. We, a group of your neighbors sincerely desiring to see our community grow better as it grows bigger, take pleasure in presenting you with this beautiful book as a memento of this most wonderful day in your lives.

On this great day you set out together as one, a deep love dwelling in your hearts, eagerly welcoming the great adventure of life. It is our sincere wish for you that God may shed His lavish blessings on the family you have founded in our midst.

In choosing your wedding gift, we felt that since books more than anything else influence the lives of people, only the best and most beautiful book was good enough for such an occasion. We confidently trust that you will find our gift a treasury of abundant inspiration throughout your married life.

The teachings of Christ, herein so beautifully portrayed, are the source of that deep, abiding happiness we wish for you. Here, too, is the wellspring of hope and consolation that sustains untold millions through life. Above all, may that love which the Master taught keep your own love fresh and new through the many years of a long and fruitful married life.

We welcome the opportunity to assist you in any way possible in your endeavor to make your marriage more and more meaningful as the years go by. Such an opportunity will be met by us in the spirit of friendly cooperation as you settle down to your new life in our community.

Portrait of Christ

for Newlyweds

*"A story, not simply to be read
and enjoyed
but to be meditated upon
and pondered,
to grasp its meaning and
magnificence"*

THE PUBLISHER

GOOD WILL PUBLISHERS, Inc.

Gastonia, North Carolina

*Printed and bound especially for
The Good Will Association, Gastonia, North Carolina*

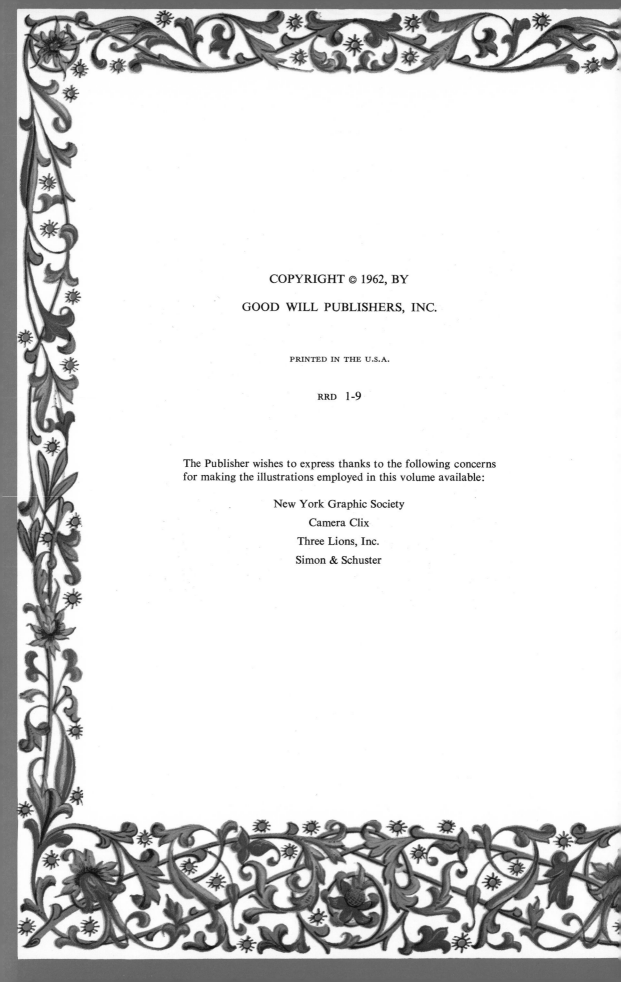

PRINTED IN THE U.S.A.

RRD 1-9

The Publisher wishes to express thanks to the following concerns
for making the illustrations employed in this volume available:

New York Graphic Society

Camera Clix

Three Lions, Inc.

Simon & Schuster

The Life of Christ

[INTRODUCTION]

THE MESSAGE of Christ's life tells us to live as we should. We do not, however, live as separate individuals but in a society. Since the family is the basic unit of society and marriage is the beginning of the family, there can be no more valuable source of instruction and help for marriage than that contained in the life of Christ.

With this in mind, we dedicate this Portrait of Christ to the newly-weds, trusting that it will help them weave Christ's message into the very fabric of their lives together, and so preserve for them the deep joy of this occasion. Life, though largely unpredictable, can bring nothing for which there is not help and advice in the life of Christ. For He is the Author of life, and lived His life amongst us as our Example and Model.

By its very nature this story is a blueprint for living and as such must be meditated on and pondered so that we can sincerely attempt to fashion our lives according to its teachings. We have, therefore, enlisted the help of many masterpieces of Christian art to add their more vivid power in capturing more fully the wealth of meaning held for us by the story of Christ's life on earth.

Such a combination of wisdom and beauty provides the newlyweds with a wedding gift most fitting to such a serious yet joyous occasion. The beauty of the gift matches the beauty of the occasion. But, most important of all, it is a practical gift, for it is the handbook of those signposts which point the way to that true happiness, which, together, in marriage you set out to find.

Gabriel Appears to Mary

THE STORY of Our Lord Jesus Christ begins with a woman, for Our Lord was truly Man as well as God. The Virgin Mary was chosen from all time to have the greatest privilege a creature could enjoy. The Second Person of the Trinity would take a body and soul like ours, be conceived in her womb, and be born of her, so that she would be the mother of Jesus. In preparation for this greatest of dignities she was highly privileged by God.

Her privilege has been beautifully expressed by Wordsworth thus:
"Mother, whose virgin bosom was uncrossed
 With the least shade of thought to sin allied,
 Woman, above all women glorified,
 Our tainted nature's solitary boast."

Mary lived in the little town of Nazareth and was betrothed to one of her countrymen named Joseph. Both were poor, showing us how little God thinks of worldly goods and social position when planning to bestow His favors on a marriage. At God's appointed time, the angel Gabriel entered Mary's home and announced to her God's plan.

The humble girl was puzzled and troubled by these words. The angel quickly reassured her however, and gently calmed her fears, before breaking the news. "Behold, thou shalt conceive in thy womb and shalt bring forth a Son, and thou shalt call his name Jesus. He shall be great and shall be called the Son of the Most High. . . ." To Mary, familiar with the prophecies of the Savior, this could mean only one thing: she was to become the mother of Christ.

Showing extraordinary prudence in the face of such astonishing news, Mary requested further explanation. She knew not man. In this wonderful girl there was not the slightest hint of prudery. Nor should there be prudery in your marriage. You are "two in one flesh" expressing your love in a way ordained by God which should exclude shame and even shyness. The angel Gabriel, matching her frankness, then told her of the divine plan, which insured that she would be the mother of the Anointed One, yet remain a Virgin.

Mary, like any other human being, was free to reject or comply with God's will. We have no grounds for assurance that, had she rejected the plan, God would have supplied an alternative arrangement for our redemption. Her glorious reply will always ring in our grateful ears—"Behold the handmaid of the Lord. Be it done unto me according to thy word."

GABRIEL APPEARS TO MARY by Bartolomé Esteban Murillo

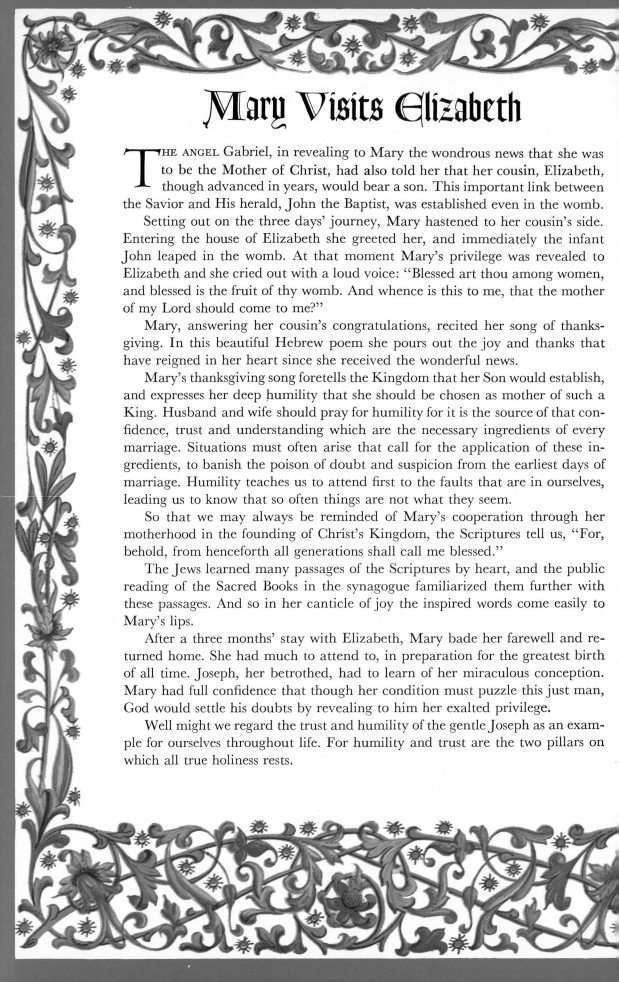

Mary Visits Elizabeth

T HE ANGEL Gabriel, in revealing to Mary the wondrous news that she was to be the Mother of Christ, had also told her that her cousin, Elizabeth, though advanced in years, would bear a son. This important link between the Savior and His herald, John the Baptist, was established even in the womb.

Setting out on the three days' journey, Mary hastened to her cousin's side. Entering the house of Elizabeth she greeted her, and immediately the infant John leaped in the womb. At that moment Mary's privilege was revealed to Elizabeth and she cried out with a loud voice: "Blessed art thou among women, and blessed is the fruit of thy womb. And whence is this to me, that the mother of my Lord should come to me?"

Mary, answering her cousin's congratulations, recited her song of thanksgiving. In this beautiful Hebrew poem she pours out the joy and thanks that have reigned in her heart since she received the wonderful news.

Mary's thanksgiving song foretells the Kingdom that her Son would establish, and expresses her deep humility that she should be chosen as mother of such a King. Husband and wife should pray for humility for it is the source of that confidence, trust and understanding which are the necessary ingredients of every marriage. Situations must often arise that call for the application of these ingredients, to banish the poison of doubt and suspicion from the earliest days of marriage. Humility teaches us to attend first to the faults that are in ourselves, leading us to know that so often things are not what they seem.

So that we may always be reminded of Mary's cooperation through her motherhood in the founding of Christ's Kingdom, the Scriptures tell us, "For, behold, from henceforth all generations shall call me blessed."

The Jews learned many passages of the Scriptures by heart, and the public reading of the Sacred Books in the synagogue familiarized them further with these passages. And so in her canticle of joy the inspired words come easily to Mary's lips.

After a three months' stay with Elizabeth, Mary bade her farewell and returned home. She had much to attend to, in preparation for the greatest birth of all time. Joseph, her betrothed, had to learn of her miraculous conception. Mary had full confidence that though her condition must puzzle this just man, God would settle his doubts by revealing to him her exalted privilege.

Well might we regard the trust and humility of the gentle Joseph as an example for ourselves throughout life. For humility and trust are the two pillars on which all true holiness rests.

MARY VISITS ELIZABETH by Carl Bloch

The Birth of Christ

SHORTLY after Mary's return from her cousin's home, the simple marriage ceremony, conducted according to Jewish custom, was completed, and Joseph led his bride to his own home, where they began their married life, a model of dedication and simplicity.

The Roman Emperor, Augustus, issued an edict that all his subject peoples register in their city of origin. The family of Joseph originated in Bethlehem, so he was obliged to make the journey there from Nazareth. Though knowing her time was near at hand, Mary, with utter trust in God, set out with him on this arduous journey. Bethlehem was, understandably, overcrowded, since many visitors had arrived for the registration. Consequently, the only shelter Joseph could find for his wife, was a little stable, probably owned by the people who conducted the inn, where they had sought admission in vain. Here in this lowly manger, Mary brought forth the King of Kings. A cold drafty stable became the centre of the universe.

God had arranged that His Son be paid homage, just after His birth, by those very dear to Christ's heart. [We shall see that throughout His life, the poor and the humble were especially favored.] As Mary and Joseph, rapt in loving devotion, bent over the Child, an angel announced the great news to a group of shepherds nearby. These tidings were not revealed to the great ones of Israel, the priests, the scholars, the Pharisees. The poor, humble, sincere shepherds were the favored ones. A chorus of angels thrilled them with their song proclaiming glory to God in heaven and peace to men on earth. Full of faith the shepherds hastened to the stable and adored the God-child, then fled to their humble homes to tell their families of the wonders they had witnessed.

The surroundings of poverty and discomfort that God chose for the birth of His Son must surely carry for us all an important message. Consistently Our Lord would teach, by word and example, the necessity of self-denial. So from His first moment on earth He would show us that though He might have chosen splendor and luxury, He chose a borrowed stable for His birth, as at death He chose a borrowed grave.

Self-denial is chosen when marriage is chosen. For marriage is not a union to ease the burdens of life, but a selfless sharing of greater responsibilities. Continually, marriage asks for self-denial and through this its deepest joys are won. For marriage soon shows us that true love is forever bound to self-denial, never counts the cost, and finds its reward in giving.

THE BIRTH OF CHRIST by J. L. Lund

The Presentation in the Temple

ON THE EIGHTH DAY following His birth, the Divine Child submitted in utter humility to the Jewish ceremony of circumcision, shedding the first drops of that blood, which would eventually flow on Calvary as a cleansing torrent. Another strict requirement of the Jewish religion was that Jesus, the first-born, be consecrated to God, and that Mary undergo the ceremony of purification. Neither He nor His mother was bound by these laws, but again setting us an example of complete obedience and humility they submitted to them.

Marriage will often call for certain things to be done which, though irksome, are part of the pattern of living. It is well to accept these things graciously rather than to set up a habit of complaint and protest in the home, where serenity and peace should reign.

Forty days after His birth, therefore, they journeyed to Jerusalem for these ceremonies. Being poor, Joseph would only be able to afford two pigeons or turtle doves, to be sacrificed by the priests, as a part of the ceremony of purification. The presentation of the Child, was a much more simple ceremony and seems to have involved no further rite than the payment of five shekels to the priests.

While they were still in the Temple, an event of deep significance took place, linking once more the Old Dispensation with the New. We find this link constantly throughout Christ's life, as in the divine plan God sought to break through the blindness of those who refused to see that Jesus Christ was indeed His Son, the Savior, promised and foretold in the Old Dispensation.

Simeon, a just and devout man, in whose heart glowed an unshakeable faith in the coming of the Savior, met Jesus, Mary and Joseph. Inspired by God, he immediately recognized Jesus as the Redeemer of Israel. Piously taking the Child from His mother's arms Simeon praised God "because my eyes have seen Thy salvation which Thou hast prepared before the face of all peoples." He then prophesied that this Child was set for the fall and rising of many. Clouding the joy, Simeon goes on to foretell the rejection of Christ by many, and warns Mary of the sword of suffering that will pierce her heart, as she shares the sufferings of her Son.

Scarcely had Simeon finished speaking when Anna, a pious widow, devoted to the service of God, approached the little group, and, inspired as was Simeon, recognized the Divine Child as the Savior. Thus, for her too, did God fulfill a lifelong desire.

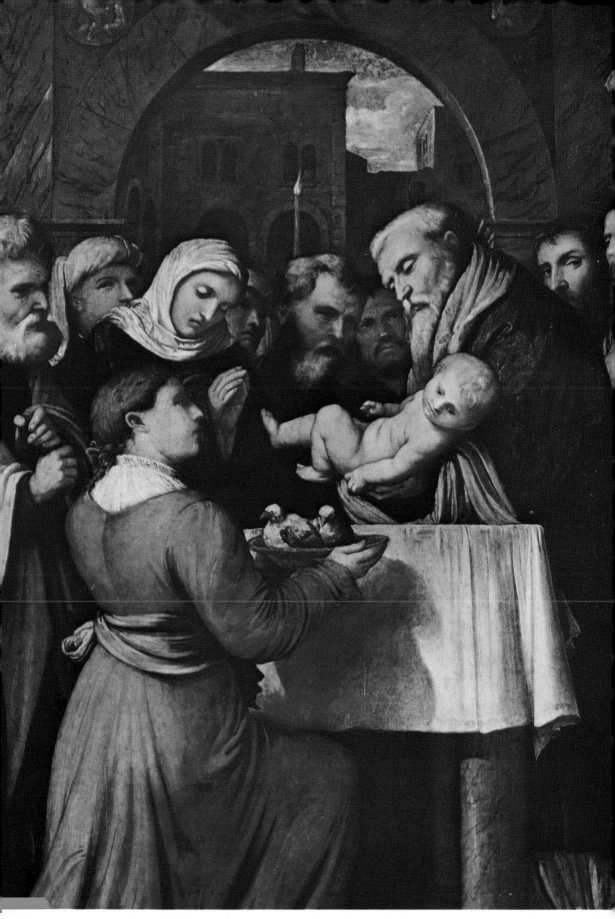

SIMEON CONFESSES JESUS AS THE SAVIOR by Girolamo di Romano

Adoration of the Wise Men

SINCE CHRIST was the King of Kings it was suitable that He should have recognition from representatives of the pagan world. And so Providence decreed that the Wise Men, scholar-priests of the Gentile world, led by the star, should come to Bethlehem to pay their respects, and adore their God. A wise husband and wife will likewise make sure that this duty is made the basis of their married life. Above all else, the creature's duty is to recognize and pay homage to the Creator.

Following the star, the Wise Men proceeded to the capital city, Jerusalem, confident of gathering there reliable information. Their simple question "Where is He that is born King of the Jews?" created great excitement. King Herod, a tyrant, and detested by his people, became alarmed immediately, for he feared he would lose the throne. He summoned the Sanhedrin, the ecclesiastical council of the Jews, and inquired of them, "Where should Christ be born?" This question the Sanhedrin answered with ease. The prophecy was quite explicit on this point. The answer was "Bethlehem." Sending for the Wise Men, Herod gave them this information and cunningly told them to report back to him later, so that he too might adore the new King.

Eventually the Wise Men located the humble dwelling of the Holy Family, acquired no doubt, when the visitors, who had come for the registration had gone back home. Oblivious of these humble surroundings, the Wise Men prostrated themselves in homage. They then presented their gifts, gold, frankincense and myrrh—frankincense, for this Child is God; gold, for He is King of Kings; myrrh, for He is man as well as God. After a short stay the Wise Men, warned by God of Herod's hypocrisy, disappeared as mysteriously as they had come.

The respect and adoration of the Wise Men, contrasted with the hatred and hypocrisy of Herod, furnishes us with an early indication of what the Child Jesus will find, when later He begins to establish His Kingdom. His own towns-folk of Nazareth will spurn Him and attempt to stone Him to death.

Often we find this too. Those nearest us, from whom we expect most help and consideration show instead callousness and even criticism. Husband and wife must use this to draw nearer to each other, matching these trials with their combined strength. Christ, though hurt by His own people never let them turn Him from His task. Nor should we let our own people affect our marriage in any way. Too often, the well-intentioned "help" offered by those close to us, fathers, mothers, brothers, sisters, can, in a subtle way, damage our marriage more than open opposition. The loyalty of husband and wife to each other is second only to loyalty to God.

THE ADORATION OF THE WISE MEN by Peter Paul Rubens

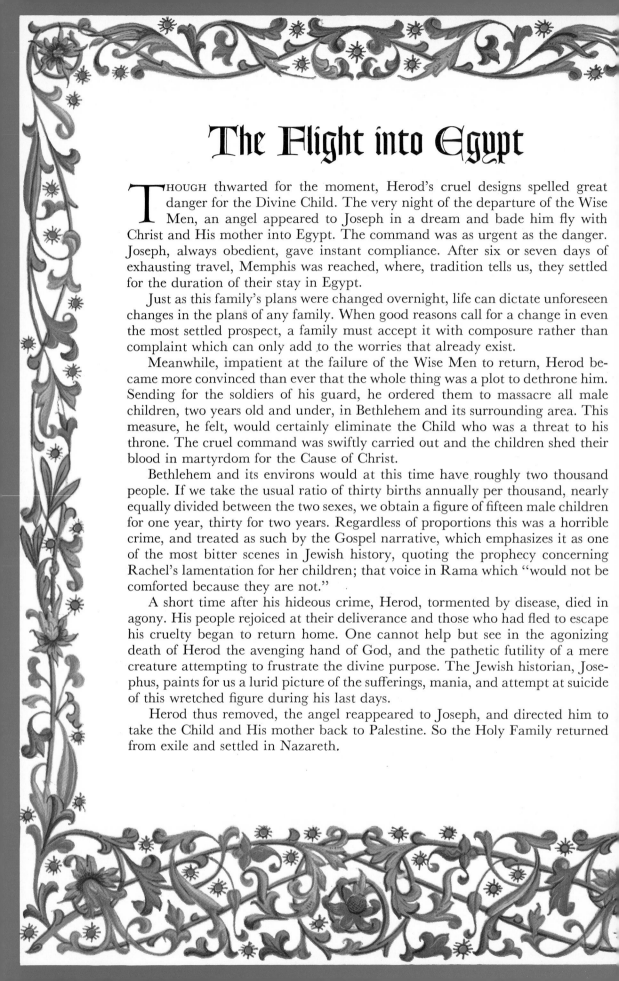

The Flight into Egypt

Though thwarted for the moment, Herod's cruel designs spelled great danger for the Divine Child. The very night of the departure of the Wise Men, an angel appeared to Joseph in a dream and bade him fly with Christ and His mother into Egypt. The command was as urgent as the danger. Joseph, always obedient, gave instant compliance. After six or seven days of exhausting travel, Memphis was reached, where, tradition tells us, they settled for the duration of their stay in Egypt.

Just as this family's plans were changed overnight, life can dictate unforeseen changes in the plans of any family. When good reasons call for a change in even the most settled prospect, a family must accept it with composure rather than complaint which can only add to the worries that already exist.

Meanwhile, impatient at the failure of the Wise Men to return, Herod became more convinced than ever that the whole thing was a plot to dethrone him. Sending for the soldiers of his guard, he ordered them to massacre all male children, two years old and under, in Bethlehem and its surrounding area. This measure, he felt, would certainly eliminate the Child who was a threat to his throne. The cruel command was swiftly carried out and the children shed their blood in martyrdom for the Cause of Christ.

Bethlehem and its environs would at this time have roughly two thousand people. If we take the usual ratio of thirty births annually per thousand, nearly equally divided between the two sexes, we obtain a figure of fifteen male children for one year, thirty for two years. Regardless of proportions this was a horrible crime, and treated as such by the Gospel narrative, which emphasizes it as one of the most bitter scenes in Jewish history, quoting the prophecy concerning Rachel's lamentation for her children; that voice in Rama which "would not be comforted because they are not."

A short time after his hideous crime, Herod, tormented by disease, died in agony. His people rejoiced at their deliverance and those who had fled to escape his cruelty began to return home. One cannot help but see in the agonizing death of Herod the avenging hand of God, and the pathetic futility of a mere creature attempting to frustrate the divine purpose. The Jewish historian, Josephus, paints for us a lurid picture of the sufferings, mania, and attempt at suicide of this wretched figure during his last days.

Herod thus removed, the angel reappeared to Joseph, and directed him to take the Child and His mother back to Palestine. So the Holy Family returned from exile and settled in Nazareth.

THE FLIGHT INTO EGYPT by Bernhard Plockhorst

The Hidden Life of Jesus

THE DIVINE plan for Jesus, when He had returned from exile and settled in Nazareth, was that He should lead a hidden life. In this small town, nestling in the hills, Jesus quietly grew to maturity, to all appearances just another normal boy, obedient and respectful to his loving parents.

The Gospel story reminds us however of His unique status by unveiling an episode of the boyhood of Jesus. As pious Jews, Mary and Joseph made the annual pilgrimage to Jerusalem to celebrate the solemn feast of the Pasch. This episode concerns the pilgrimage made by them when Jesus was twelve years old.

After the celebration of the feast, which lasted for a week, when the caravan was about to start on the return journey, Mary and Joseph discovered that Jesus was missing. Amidst the noise and bustle of the caravan preparing to leave, they inquired anxiously of Him. He might be with their relatives or friends. But the caravan was under way now and still there was no sign of Him. Sorrowfully, they decided to make the return journey to Jerusalem to search for Him there. At last, on the third day, they found Him in the Temple, sitting amongst the doctors, and astounding them with His wisdom. Before him, in a semi-circle, sat the venerable rabbis craning forward in their eagerness as this young Boy so masterfully took charge of the discussion. The Talmud assures us that such discussion was common. But a boy of twelve, questioning and answering with such a depth of wisdom was indeed unique. With complete composure and no trace of shyness Jesus expounded the Scriptures with a clarity and understanding startling to these men who had a lifetime's training and experience in this very subject.

Perplexed by the whole incident, first by the sudden disappearance of so dutiful a son, now by finding him in such a scene, His mother gently asked for an explanation, telling Him of the sorrow and anxiety that had been caused Joseph and herself. In answer, Jesus simply reminded His mother that He was performing a task allotted Him by His Father in heaven; and of the many things He must do as Teacher of mankind.

Jesus then obediently returned with them to Nazareth, where, for the next eighteen years, He was subject to them. Constantly, as our Model, He set for us a pattern and example of love, humility and obedience.

This episode has much to teach us about family life. On the one hand, Mary, though hurt and worried by Christ's disappearance, did not scold but gently asked her Child for an explanation. On the other hand, Jesus showed perfect respect and obedience. In our times, insistence on obedience is often represented as an attempt to distort a child's personality. The folly of such thinking is exposed by the example given us by Christ as a Child.

JESUS AT TWELVE by Heinrich Hofmann

The Coming of John the Baptist

Throughout their whole history the Jews clung to their great hope, the promise of the Savior. This was the cornerstone of their culture, their support in the midst of all the trials and tribulations witnessed by their race. Again and again their prophets had foretold it. They knew the poetry of the prophecies by heart, telling of the herald who would come before the King, preparing His way. "The voice of one crying in the wilderness. Prepare ye the way of the Lord."

John the Baptist was well known to many. His father was a prominent man and the circumstances of John the Baptist's birth were still remembered. His life as a hermit was in itself a fascination to people. Now he had emerged from his solitude and preached the coming of Christ, in fulfillment of his role as herald bearing witness of the Light through Whom all men might believe. The spiritual leaders of the Jews had always been particular about their dress, and punctilious in their attention to the letter of the law. John the Baptist clothed himself with whatever came readily to hand, a garment of camel's hair for instance. In his preaching he broke through the details of the Law and sought to reach the very hearts of men.

After the harvest season, probably in October, we find Jesus emerging from His hidden life. The news of John the Baptist's preaching had reached Galilee, and a group set out along the Jordan on their way to hear him. One member of this group was Jesus, known to His townsmen as a carpenter. At the Jordan ford He, with the others, stopped to listen. With these others, unassuming as ever, He stepped forward to be baptized, last of the group. John the Baptist did not at first know who He was, so perfect was Our Lord's humility. Yet, even before God revealed it to him, he knew that this Man should be the one baptizing. This was the One for whom he was herald. Our Lord, however, meek and submissive, overcame his protests and insisted on being baptized.

Showing submission on his part, His herald obeyed. After the baptism, when Jesus had stepped from the water, the Holy Spirit descended on Him in the form of a dove, and a voice from heaven said, "This is my beloved Son in whom I am well pleased."

Often in married life there is the temptation to be anything but submissive. Foolishly, we think that a constant insistence on our rights is a sign of strength, whereas love teaches that it is but weakness. When husband and wife truly put the other first, forgetting self, then all that is due is given and received automatically.

THE BAPTISM OF JESUS by Christian Dalsgaard

The Samaritan Woman

After his baptism, Our Lord went to a desert region and remained there fasting and praying for forty days. The hidden life was over. Now He prepared for His public life amongst His people. Satan, aware of approaching salvation through Christ, must use every weapon in his armory to stave off defeat. Jesus answered his temptations with a declaration of war, and sent him scurrying to defeat.

Two months after His baptism the Master's ministry began. One day, walking by the side of the Jordan He met John the Baptist who proclaimed Him "Lamb of God." Next day Jesus returned, and again John the Baptist proclaimed Him: "Behold the Lamb of God," and two of his disciples, Galileans, rose and followed Christ. Turning to them, Our Lord said, "What seek you?" Spontaneously, they answered "Rabbi," indicating that they accepted Him as their Master. Jesus invited them to come with Him to His little hut which stood by the bend of the river.

Next day, Andrew, who was one of the two, brought back Simon his brother. Before he could be introduced Jesus said, "Thou art Simon the son of Jona. Thou shalt be called Cephas." In this way Andrew and Simon, or Peter, became the first two disciples. Very soon, Philip and Nathaniel joined them, and later the rest of the Twelve.

All was now ready. Now the Master would go forth to teach. Now He would work miracles that His people might believe in Him. He chose as the scene of His first public miracle a wedding feast at Cana, where in answer to His mother's request He changed water into wine. The choice of a wedding ceremony as the occasion for His first miracle reminds us of Christ's high esteem for marriage; an example of the esteem in which we must always hold our marriage.

A year had passed and Christ continued to preach and baptize. The picture was not very bright, for though His followers had grown in number, Herod had thrown John the Baptist into prison, and the people of Judea had shown poor response to the Savior.

One day travelling through Samaria with His disciples, Jesus stopped by a well to rest. His own people regarded the Samaritans as heretics and a bitter rivalry had grown up between them. A Samaritan woman came to the well to draw water. Convention forbade His talking to her, but He asked her for a drink and conversed with her. Soon, through His gentle guidance, she confessed Him the Savior.

Christ's forgiveness and tolerance, shown to this woman, points the way to that foregiveness and tolerance that is needed in every marriage. Often, since we are human, husband and wife will need the forgiveness of the other for many faults, great and small. Pride, in the form of blindness to our own faults, is the greatest obstacle to our forgiveness and tolerance of faults in the other.

JESUS AND THE SAMARITAN WOMAN by Carl Bloch

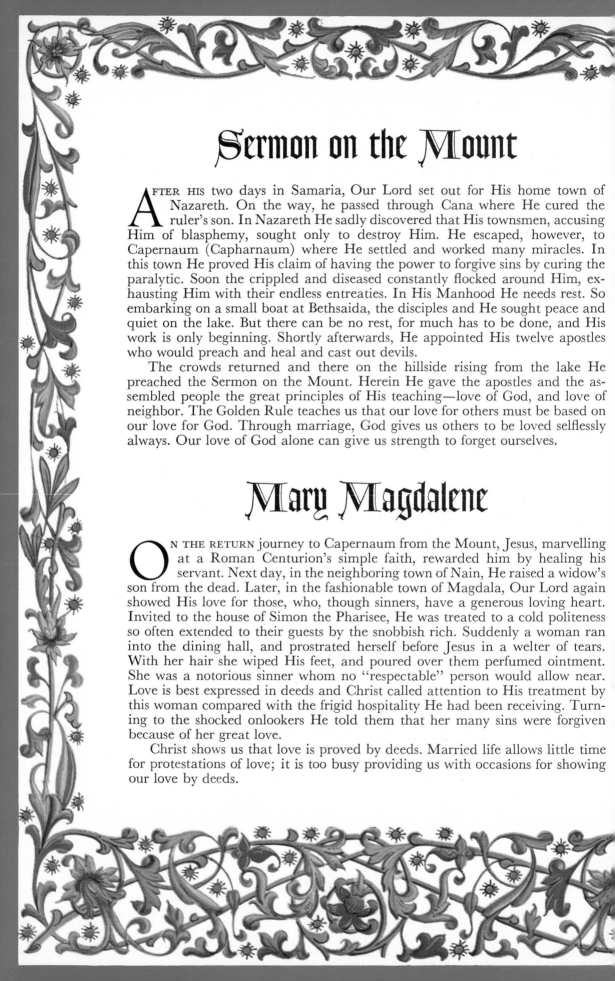

Sermon on the Mount

AFTER HIS two days in Samaria, Our Lord set out for His home town of Nazareth. On the way, he passed through Cana where He cured the ruler's son. In Nazareth He sadly discovered that His townsmen, accusing Him of blasphemy, sought only to destroy Him. He escaped, however, to Capernaum (Capharnaum) where He settled and worked many miracles. In this town He proved His claim of having the power to forgive sins by curing the paralytic. Soon the crippled and diseased constantly flocked around Him, exhausting Him with their endless entreaties. In His Manhood He needs rest. So embarking on a small boat at Bethsaida, the disciples and He sought peace and quiet on the lake. But there can be no rest, for much has to be done, and His work is only beginning. Shortly afterwards, He appointed His twelve apostles who would preach and heal and cast out devils.

The crowds returned and there on the hillside rising from the lake He preached the Sermon on the Mount. Herein He gave the apostles and the assembled people the great principles of His teaching—love of God, and love of neighbor. The Golden Rule teaches us that our love for others must be based on our love for God. Through marriage, God gives us others to be loved selflessly always. Our love of God alone can give us strength to forget ourselves.

Mary Magdalene

ON THE RETURN journey to Capernaum from the Mount, Jesus, marvelling at a Roman Centurion's simple faith, rewarded him by healing his servant. Next day, in the neighboring town of Nain, He raised a widow's son from the dead. Later, in the fashionable town of Magdala, Our Lord again showed His love for those, who, though sinners, have a generous loving heart. Invited to the house of Simon the Pharisee, He was treated to a cold politeness so often extended to their guests by the snobbish rich. Suddenly a woman ran into the dining hall, and prostrated herself before Jesus in a welter of tears. With her hair she wiped His feet, and poured over them perfumed ointment. She was a notorious sinner whom no "respectable" person would allow near. Love is best expressed in deeds and Christ called attention to His treatment by this woman compared with the frigid hospitality He had been receiving. Turning to the shocked onlookers He told them that her many sins were forgiven because of her great love.

Christ shows us that love is proved by deeds. Married life allows little time for protestations of love; it is too busy providing us with occasions for showing our love by deeds.

JESUS LOVES THOSE WHO LOVE by Anton Dorph

Jesus Calms the Storm

AS WAS HIS practice, when exhausted by His labours, Our Lord sought a few hours peace on the lake. This lake, or sea, of Galilee is about fourteen miles long from north to south, and about six miles across at its broadest part. Suddenly a freak wind hit the small craft, threatening to capsize it. The Master lay asleep, untroubled. His apostles were in panic. They frantically wakened Him, and He immediately quelled the storm. Then He chided them for their poor faith, again reminding them that His followers needed before all else a strong and firm faith in the Master.

A marriage is very like a small craft sailing through the sea of life. Often the sea is smooth, but often too it is turbulent. Waves of troubles threaten to engulf our marriage which seems so flimsy on the sea of life. Shoals of sickness, poverty, misfortune, menace us. But a firm faith alone is needed; for that will calm the most dangerous storm of all—the storm within our breasts—enabling us to steer surely through every danger.

Next morning, they put in at Gerasa where He drove out the unclean spirit sending it into a herd of swine. Scarcely rested, they re-crossed the lake and returned to His beloved Capernaum. More miracles were to come. He cured the woman with the issue of blood and raised the daughter of Jairus to life. Now His fame was widespread throughout the countryside; nevertheless, when He returned to Nazareth, He found His townsmen still rejected Him. Nazareth would never be given another opportunity.

Another tour of Galilee served to show the disciples the fields white for the harvest and to prepare them for the work that lay ahead. Having instructed them, Our Lord sent them forth to teach and preach in the cities while He returned to Capernaum to pray for them. On His journey He received the sad news of John the Baptist's beheading by Herod. What suffering must have flooded His heart, for not only did He know that John alone amongst men fully understood Him and His work, but also that this marked the opening of warfare on Himself.

Soon, the Twelve returned, bubbling with enthusiasm in their accounts of their work. How they must have looked forward to the Master's commendation and further advice. But once more the crowds pressed, and to escape them they took ship to a desert place to rest. But there was no escape. The crowds followed the sail to meet Him where He landed. His heart touched by this devotion, He came ashore and taught them. Here he worked the miracle of the loaves and fishes. Thwarting their efforts to make Him king, Our Lord bade the apostles to take ship for Bethsaida, while He dismissed the people. That night, again showing them the importance of faith, He came walking over the water to join them as they sailed.

JESUS AND THE FISHERMEN by Ernst Zimmermann

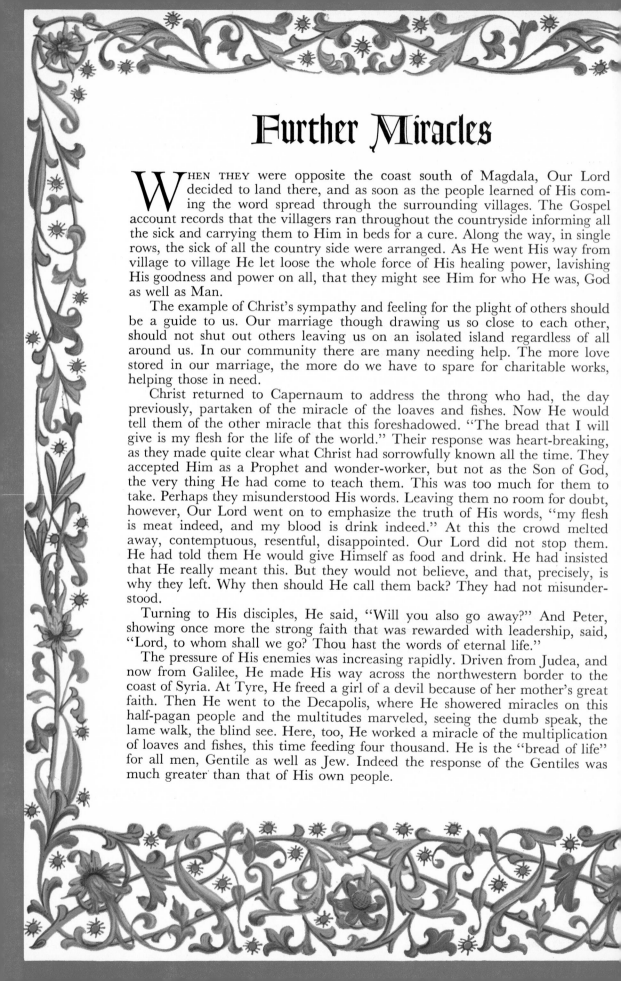

Further Miracles

WHEN THEY were opposite the coast south of Magdala, Our Lord decided to land there, and as soon as the people learned of His coming the word spread through the surrounding villages. The Gospel account records that the villagers ran throughout the countryside informing all the sick and carrying them to Him in beds for a cure. Along the way, in single rows, the sick of all the country side were arranged. As He went His way from village to village He let loose the whole force of His healing power, lavishing His goodness and power on all, that they might see Him for who He was, God as well as Man.

The example of Christ's sympathy and feeling for the plight of others should be a guide to us. Our marriage though drawing us so close to each other, should not shut out others leaving us on an isolated island regardless of all around us. In our community there are many needing help. The more love stored in our marriage, the more do we have to spare for charitable works, helping those in need.

Christ returned to Capernaum to address the throng who had, the day previously, partaken of the miracle of the loaves and fishes. Now He would tell them of the other miracle that this foreshadowed. "The bread that I will give is my flesh for the life of the world." Their response was heart-breaking, as they made quite clear what Christ had sorrowfully known all the time. They accepted Him as a Prophet and wonder-worker, but not as the Son of God, the very thing He had come to teach them. This was too much for them to take. Perhaps they misunderstood His words. Leaving them no room for doubt, however, Our Lord went on to emphasize the truth of His words, "my flesh is meat indeed, and my blood is drink indeed." At this the crowd melted away, contemptuous, resentful, disappointed. Our Lord did not stop them. He had told them He would give Himself as food and drink. He had insisted that He really meant this. But they would not believe, and that, precisely, is why they left. Why then should He call them back? They had not misunderstood.

Turning to His disciples, He said, "Will you also go away?" And Peter, showing once more the strong faith that was rewarded with leadership, said, "Lord, to whom shall we go? Thou hast the words of eternal life."

The pressure of His enemies was increasing rapidly. Driven from Judea, and now from Galilee, He made His way across the northwestern border to the coast of Syria. At Tyre, He freed a girl of a devil because of her mother's great faith. Then He went to the Decapolis, where He showered miracles on this half-pagan people and the multitudes marveled, seeing the dumb speak, the lame walk, the blind see. Here, too, He worked a miracle of the multiplication of loaves and fishes, this time feeding four thousand. He is the "bread of life" for all men, Gentile as well as Jew. Indeed the response of the Gentiles was much greater than that of His own people.

JESUS HEALING THE SICK by Gabriel Max

Jesus Restores Sight to the Blind

AFTER HIS sojourn in Syria, Our Lord directed the Twelve to set sail, not for Capernaum as they had expected, but to a point further south, the Jordan ford. While they were resting here, the Pharisees and Sadducees came to talk with Him. But He was weary of their pretence and hypocrisy. There is no one so blind as the man who does not want to see. Husbands and wives should remember that love is not blind as cynics often say. Rather does it see beyond appearances with the eyes of trust and understanding.

The little party set sail for the north again and eventually put in at Bethsaida. The townsfolk, anxious to see more wonders, had a blind man in mind; they would now produce him and have him cured. So they brought forward the afflicted one and presented him to Jesus.

Our Lord, eternally patient, took him by the hand and led him outside the town. Taking a little spittle, He spread it over the blind man's eyes, who at once began to see in a shadowy fashion. Then the Master placed His hands over the eyes, and the man who had been blind began to see all things clearly.

That afternoon, Jesus, with the Twelve, left Bethsaida and went northwards to Caesarea Philippi. He wanted to be alone to pray, and He had important things to discuss with His disciples. Constantly we find Christ slipping off by Himself to commune with the Father, and in this manner Scripture tells us that, during this journey He continued all night in prayer to God. Throughout the hurry and bustle of family life time always must be found for prayer. Every marriage needs the interior help and strength of regular prayer to instill that spiritual force into our lives without which everything is meaningless. Without prayer, worldliness eats into our souls and sows restlessness and dissatisfaction with all the temptations that threaten our marriage and family.

In the morning, Jesus gathered the Twelve around Him; now He would give them, after all they had seen, the final test of faith. He began by asking what men thought of Him, who He was. They had lived close to Him, seen His miracles and heard His teaching. What would be their answer? Would they be like the others and think of Him only as a wonder-worker, or another prophet?

They first gave Him the current opinions on such a question. Then He asked their own opinion. Again Simon Peter, in his limitless faith, spoke for them.

"Thou are the Christ, the Son of the living God."

The impetuous Simon loved and believed in Him. There were others more prudent, but none loved Christ more. The Master's reply was Peter's reward for such love and trust: "Thou art Peter, and upon this rock I will build my Church."

JESUS HEALING THE BLIND by Martimus Rorbye

The Transfiguration

THE DAY OF Simon Peter's confession was a landmark. Christ had come to found a Kingdom, and that day the foundation stone had been firmly laid. Now He led the apostles back to Galilee. Despite His knowledge of what lay ahead, there was a firm note of confidence in His preaching. Love and self-denial were the qualities required in anyone who would follow Him.

How well these two qualities, love and self-denial, sum up all that is needed for a happy marriage as they do for a follower of Christ. That is so, precisely because true happiness can only be achieved through the teachings of Christ. Love without self-denial is romantic nonsense. Self-denial without love is worthless.

From the outskirts of Capernaum His little band moved southward to Mount Tabor (Thabor). Taking Peter, James and John, He climbed the steep slopes to the summit, and went aside to pray. His companions, though well intentioned, but weary with the climb, fell asleep. But soon they were awakened. They had made their ascent in the evening, and by now it was night, yet around them glowed light brighter than day. Focusing their eyes with difficulty, they saw that the light came from the spot where Jesus had knelt down to pray. But now a figure stood there. It was Jesus, yet he looked so different! The light coming from Him was as brilliant and blinding as the light from the sun. His clothes glittered whiter than snow. Though dazzled by the sight, they gradually perceived that Christ was conversing with Moses and Elias. Then it was all over. Jesus touched them, melting their fear and awe.

Meanwhile, the other nine apostles had had a disappointing time. They had tried to cure a demoniac boy and had failed. Jesus instructed the boy's father that all things are possible to him who believes, and in response to the father's belief the son was cured. Then He patiently taught His disciples that their faith must be yet firmer, and that often there was need of prayer and fasting to carry out their work of healing.

Thence He passed on secretly to Galilee. Secretly, for His enemies sought to kill Him, and He had much still to do before delivering Himself into their hands. After many months in Galilee, spent in training His disciples, He once more set out for Capernaum. No longer was He a popular figure. Suspicion and resentment were His welcome. Settled here, He had the time to continue His training of the Twelve. But not for long, for His work had to be resumed. Though humanly shrinking from it, He had to go up to Jerusalem for the Feast of the Tabernacles. Now the last battle was about to start, closing with His death and resurrection.

JESUS ASKED LOVE AND BELIEF by Heinrich Hofmann

The Good Shepherd

DURING THIS stay in Jerusalem the Pharisees and His other enemies used every trick to trap Him. They brought to Him a woman accused of adultery, knowing His merciful treatment of such people. Citing the law of Moses they asked what His sentence would be. He quietly told them, "He that is without sin among you let him first cast a stone." Baffled once more, they slunk away. Thus does Our Lord deal with insincerity. And so the endless argumentation continued. The Pharisees drove the gentle Jesus to label them as a "generation of vipers." At last, since they continued to avoid the issue, He declared His divinity, using the strongest possible emphasis, "Before Abraham was, I am." This was quite clear. There could be no further room for doubt. Jesus Christ is God. They took up stones to stone Him to death, but Jesus escaped, for His hour had not yet come.

The insincerity of the Pharisees, beyond all else, provoked Christ's wrath. Insincerity in marriage is fatal, for it destroys all grounds for mutual trust. Lies and falsity of any kind must breed suspicion and kill respect. Love can cope with anything but hypocrisy.

At the close of this troubled week in Jerusalem, Jesus led His friends to a nearby hillside, and expounded the parable of the Good Shepherd. We have here a fine example of how Our Lord used His surroundings to illustrate His teaching. It was the latter part of the autumn, and the rainy season was fast approaching. The sheep were scattered over the bare hills, nibbling at the scanty pasture. Every evening the shepherd came and counted them, calling each by name as he gathered them into the folds for the night. In his little hut nearby he kept constant vigil to protect them against thieves and desert beasts. In this beautiful teaching the Master explains that He is the Good Shepherd, ready to lay down His life for us, His sheep. Others, who do not accept Him, are nevertheless His sheep too, and these must be brought into the fold so that there be one fold and one Shepherd.

When He left Jerusalem, we find that Our Lord moved from place to place so that it is hard to keep track of His whereabouts. It is as though He would not remain long in any one place during the next five months of His life so that in this way He might escape danger, for He would only deliver Himself at the appointed time. We are told that during this period He chose seventy-two disciples to promote His teaching and sent them out on His work. They returned joyously to Him to give Him a report of their success, and enjoy the reward of His boundless gratitude and congratulations.

THE GOOD SHEPHERD by Bernhard Plockhorst

Quibbling about the Sabbath

URING THIS time we find a lawyer questioning Jesus on His teaching. For the simple people the Master has always a warm welcome. This man is a legalist, most precise, full of objections. Our Lord takes him on his own terms, handles him masterfully and finally silences him with the parable of the Good Samaritan. In this way He showed the lawyer that His teaching is not the subject for complicated legal analysis. Summed up it is quite simple: love God, and love your neighbor.

We next find Christ in Bethany, at the house of His great friends, Lazarus, Martha and Mary. About this time, a certain Pharisee invited Our Lord to dinner. Courteous as ever to these people, despite their sham and humbug, He accepted. Again the legalists, with their hollow hair-splitting, kept maneuvering to condemn Him out of His own mouth. Again, however, with dignified authority, He tore their flimsy arguments to shreds and tried to shake them out of their perilous complacency.

In marriage it is important that our lives be run in an orderly fashion. But there is, for some people, the danger of pursuing order and detail for their own sake, which can quickly ruin the whole spirit of marriage and give rise to petty bickering and quibbling. A readiness to suit the reasonable requirements of the other should underlie every household schedule.

For the next few months it would seem that Jesus planned to confine Himself to the country on either side of the Jordan ford. Teaching in a synagogue on a Sabbath day, He cured a woman who suffered from a disease that bent her almost double. The quibble arose, not for the first time, of healing on the Sabbath. Again He silenced this hypocrisy by pointing out that it was never unlawful to do a good work. Later, again on a Sabbath day, He accepted the invitation of a certain Pharisee to dine with him, knowing full well that this offer of hospitality only masked another attempt to trap Him no matter what His approach might be.

Jesus realized that in dealing with such people one's patience has a double trial; first, in that they play false, and secondly in that one has to endure their gloating over fancied success. Their falsity He would endure, but never would He let them think they had deceived Him, for He always strove to save them from themselves.

In the corner of the dining room was a dropsical man. Obviously they had arranged this as a test case, and wanted to see if He would heal this man on the Sabbath, now that He knew how strongly they opposed this. Legalists to the end, they wanted to see what He would do and condemn Him for it, no matter what course He followed. Jesus ignored them, got up from the table, cured the sick man and gently told him to go home. Resignedly, and with vast patience, He once more justified His actions, ever hopeful that He might reach their hearts, hard as they were.

JESUS DESTROYED HYPOCRISY by Heinrich Hofmann

The Raising of Lazarus

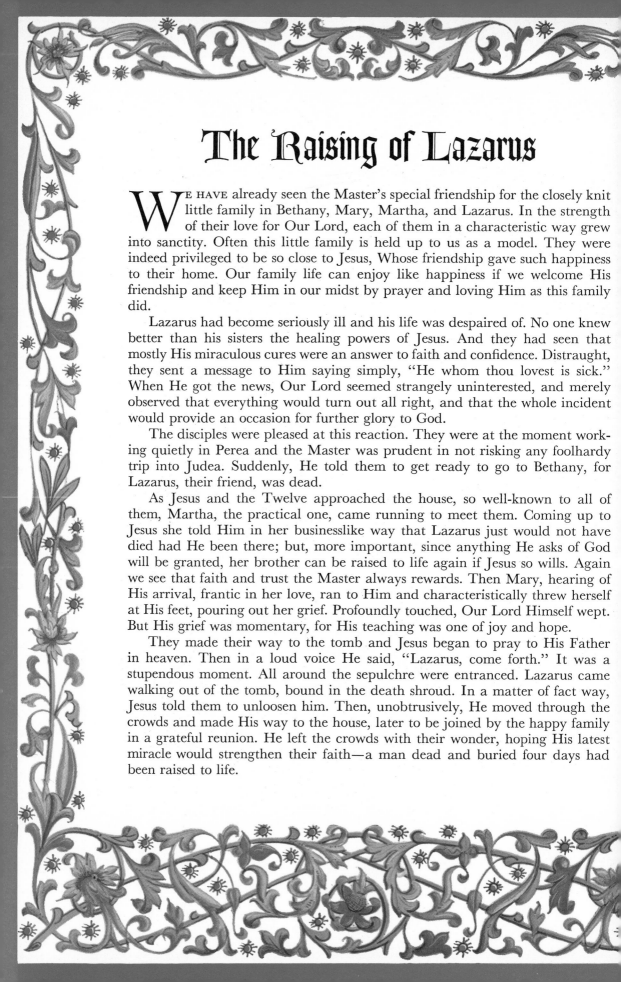

WE HAVE already seen the Master's special friendship for the closely knit little family in Bethany, Mary, Martha, and Lazarus. In the strength of their love for Our Lord, each of them in a characteristic way grew into sanctity. Often this little family is held up to us as a model. They were indeed privileged to be so close to Jesus, Whose friendship gave such happiness to their home. Our family life can enjoy like happiness if we welcome His friendship and keep Him in our midst by prayer and loving Him as this family did.

Lazarus had become seriously ill and his life was despaired of. No one knew better than his sisters the healing powers of Jesus. And they had seen that mostly His miraculous cures were an answer to faith and confidence. Distraught, they sent a message to Him saying simply, "He whom thou lovest is sick." When He got the news, Our Lord seemed strangely uninterested, and merely observed that everything would turn out all right, and that the whole incident would provide an occasion for further glory to God.

The disciples were pleased at this reaction. They were at the moment working quietly in Perea and the Master was prudent in not risking any foolhardy trip into Judea. Suddenly, He told them to get ready to go to Bethany, for Lazarus, their friend, was dead.

As Jesus and the Twelve approached the house, so well-known to all of them, Martha, the practical one, came running to meet them. Coming up to Jesus she told Him in her businesslike way that Lazarus just would not have died had He been there; but, more important, since anything He asks of God will be granted, her brother can be raised to life again if Jesus so wills. Again we see that faith and trust the Master always rewards. Then Mary, hearing of His arrival, frantic in her love, ran to Him and characteristically threw herself at His feet, pouring out her grief. Profoundly touched, Our Lord Himself wept. But His grief was momentary, for His teaching was one of joy and hope.

They made their way to the tomb and Jesus began to pray to His Father in heaven. Then in a loud voice He said, "Lazarus, come forth." It was a stupendous moment. All around the sepulchre were entranced. Lazarus came walking out of the tomb, bound in the death shroud. In a matter of fact way, Jesus told them to unloosen him. Then, unobtrusively, He moved through the crowds and made His way to the house, later to be joined by the happy family in a grateful reunion. He left the crowds with their wonder, hoping His latest miracle would strengthen their faith—a man dead and buried four days had been raised to life.

THE RAISING OF LAZARUS by Carl Bloch

Jesus and the Children

THOUGH MANY believed through the miracle of the raising of Lazarus, many were still unconvinced. But the chief priests and Pharisees were afraid of Our Lord's mounting importance and influence. Caiaphas (Caiphas), high-priest of this year, presided at a council meeting to discuss the problem. They decided that the Romans would soon tire of strife and faction amongst the Jewish people, and restrict further what liberty was left to them as a subject people. The interests of the Jewish nation required that Jesus must die. It was for them an easy decision. On hearing the sentence, Jesus, with the Twelve, went to a quiet little town called Ephraim. Here He would hide meantime. Soon He would deliver Himself to them.

At length the day came for setting out on His last journey to Jerusalem. On His way through Galilee the multitudes flocked to Him once more, and He taught them and healed many sick. On the outskirts of a little town in Galilee, He cured the ten lepers. Only one came back to thank Him. He had showered favors on so many, during His life, yet gratitude had been so seldom returned.

This utter love and tenderness of Our Lord we see highlighted in the touching scene of Jesus and the children that took place on this last journey to Jerusalem. A number of women pushed through the crowds to have Him bless their children. The Twelve, feeling very important, now that Jesus was popular with the people, coldly turned the mothers aside, telling them that the Master was much too busy with more important matters. Jesus noticed what was going on. Lovingly, He gathered the children to Him and gently embraced them. The little ones nestled up to Him, their faces shining with love and trust. As they clung to Him in their love, He called the Twelve and sharply reproved them for trying to keep the children from him. This was yet another lesson they had to learn. They might have saved themselves this reproof, for they had seen His love for the poor, straightforward, simple people, and His detestation of the scheming diplomacy of the worldly-wise. All He asked was a childlike sincerity and trust. "Suffer little children to come unto me . . . for of such is the kingdom of God."

Christ's great love for children highlights that privilege which, normally, is granted through our marriage, the begetting and bringing up of children. As God, He entrusts to us these little ones whom He loves so much, and always we should discharge our rights and duties as mother and father in this light, counting it the high honor it so truly is. Often, they will demand self-sacrifice which is the unfailing test of true love. But always the rewards are great, even in this life, for through children the love of the parents is perpetuated in a way that God alone could arrange.

SUFFER LITTLE CHILDREN TO COME UNTO ME by Bernhard Plockhorst

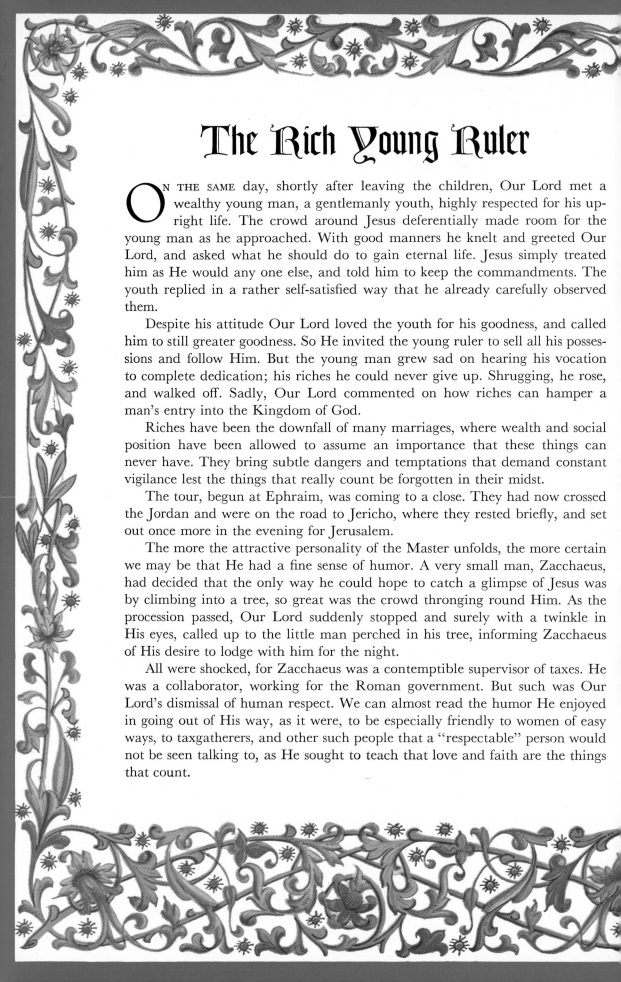

The Rich Young Ruler

ON THE SAME day, shortly after leaving the children, Our Lord met a wealthy young man, a gentlemanly youth, highly respected for his upright life. The crowd around Jesus deferentially made room for the young man as he approached. With good manners he knelt and greeted Our Lord, and asked what he should do to gain eternal life. Jesus simply treated him as He would any one else, and told him to keep the commandments. The youth replied in a rather self-satisfied way that he already carefully observed them.

Despite his attitude Our Lord loved the youth for his goodness, and called him to still greater goodness. So He invited the young ruler to sell all his possessions and follow Him. But the young man grew sad on hearing his vocation to complete dedication; his riches he could never give up. Shrugging, he rose, and walked off. Sadly, Our Lord commented on how riches can hamper a man's entry into the Kingdom of God.

Riches have been the downfall of many marriages, where wealth and social position have been allowed to assume an importance that these things can never have. They bring subtle dangers and temptations that demand constant vigilance lest the things that really count be forgotten in their midst.

The tour, begun at Ephraim, was coming to a close. They had now crossed the Jordan and were on the road to Jericho, where they rested briefly, and set out once more in the evening for Jerusalem.

The more the attractive personality of the Master unfolds, the more certain we may be that He had a fine sense of humor. A very small man, Zacchaeus, had decided that the only way he could hope to catch a glimpse of Jesus was by climbing into a tree, so great was the crowd thronging round Him. As the procession passed, Our Lord suddenly stopped and surely with a twinkle in His eyes, called up to the little man perched in his tree, informing Zacchaeus of His desire to lodge with him for the night.

All were shocked, for Zacchaeus was a contemptible supervisor of taxes. He was a collaborator, working for the Roman government. But such was Our Lord's dismissal of human respect. We can almost read the humor He enjoyed in going out of His way, as it were, to be especially friendly to women of easy ways, to taxgatherers, and other such people that a "respectable" person would not be seen talking to, as He sought to teach that love and faith are the things that count.

THE RICH YOUNG RULER by Heinrich Hofmann

Palm Sunday

AFTER HIS visit with Zacchaeus, Jesus proceeded to Bethany. Here He attended a banquet given in His honor by Simon the Leper, a man cured of this disease by Our Lord. During this banquet the everloving Mary Magdalene anointed His feet with expensive ointment. Judas' criticism that this was sheer extravagance the Master sharply rebuked.

Next morning, preparing to leave Bethany, Jesus sent two disciples to Bethphage to fetch Him an ass and its colt. Thus would His entry into Jerusalem fulfill the prophecy foretelling the coming of the King. He would be poor and riding on an ass.

Surrounded by the people of Bethany, He began the journey to Jerusalem. The excitement mounted rapidly as the procession approached the gate and crowds poured out to meet them. Palm tree boughs were ripped down and strewn on the road before Him, and the wildly enthusiastic throng shouted their praise and welcome. Orders had been published that Jesus be arrested on sight, but the priests cringed into the background. Such popular acclaim they had not reckoned with.

The Moneychangers Expelled

THE NIGHT following the triumphal entry into Jerusalem was spent quietly in Bethany. Next day Our Lord returned to the Temple. Two years before, at the Pasch, He had driven the traffickers from the sacred enclosure with a whip braided of cords. Since then these men had returned to their old ways, encouraged by the priests and the ancients. The moneychangers, seated at their tables, were again in their former places. Nearby were the sellers of doves for the sacrifices. The din of voices raised in bargaining rang out through the whole sanctuary.

Once more Jesus impressed His authority as He turned over their tables with His foot, and drove them before Him from the Temple courts. How dare they desecrate the house of God! "My house shall be called the house of prayer; but ye have made it a den of thieves."

In our times, business is allowed to intrude into phases of our lives which should remain untouched. Men often become comparative strangers to their wives and families because of the claims of business. Mothers often take jobs to improve the family income when doing with less in the home would show greater wisdom in the matter of family life. Our values in marriage should never be disturbed by the trend of our times.

JESUS DRIVING MONEYLENDERS FROM THE TEMPLE by Carl Bloch

Render unto Caesar

RETURNING again to the Temple on Tuesday, Jesus resumed His teaching. Never before had His teaching been received with such popular enthusiasm, so that the chief priest and scribes felt more and more helpless. But at all costs they must attempt to quell His rising popularity, so again they questioned Him on the authority He now so openly assumed. Again Jesus was patient with them, and tried to show them their folly through parables. The parables they refused to apply to themselves, no matter how obvious Jesus made it that they were aimed directly at them.

By this time, thoroughly alarmed, and growing more fearful by the hour, the Pharisees opened up a new line of attack. They would seek to embroil Jesus with the secular authority, and cause Him to antagonize the Roman Governor. Slyly, affecting that they had almost been won over, they asked Him, "Is it lawful for us to give tribute to Caesar?"

Compulsion to pay taxes to their Roman overlords rankled strongly with the proud Jews. Furthermore, as dutiful observers of the Law of Moses, should they not resist this ordinance? If Jesus told them not to pay taxes, the Romans would immediately deal with Him. If He told them to pay taxes, the Pharisees would point out that He was not a loyal Jew. Such was the dilemma that these men in their cunning hypocrisy posed for Our Lord.

He knew their trickery and insincerity; so their dilemma He would answer with subtlety, and avoid implicating Himself. He asked for a coin and was handed a penny or a denarius, a little silver coin worth about fourteen cents. Taking the coin in His hand, He asked them, "Whose image and inscription is this?" They answered "Caesar's." As He handed back the coin to its owner, Our Lord simply said, "Render therefore unto Caesar the things that are Caesar's and unto God the things that are God's."

His reply was short and to the point. It showed them that He had not been for a moment deluded by their assumed simplicity. He did not lose His temper with their finesse and paltry diplomacy. He simply called their bluff, and exposed their half-truths for what they were.

In His answer, Christ neatly stated the fact that we must recognize two authorities, God and the state. The family unit, which we begin through marriage, is of first importance in our society, for as the state exists to serve the family, so the family has corresponding duties towards the state. Good citizenship is, then, a Christian duty to be fulfilled in a responsible way, with an active interest in the governing of our community and country.

RENDER UNTO CAESAR by Anton Dorph

The Last Supper

THE SANHEDRIN, a council composed of chief priests, Scribes and elders, having now finally rejected Jesus, met that night in the house of Caiaphas. Christ's popularity constrained them to take Him secretly. Thus did Judas, the traitor, play into their hands by his offer to betray the Master. They agreed to pay him thirty shekels, about seventeen dollars, for his treachery.

Wednesday passed without incident. Early Thursday morning, the day of the Pasch, Jesus sent Peter and John to Jerusalem to find a room and prepare for the paschal meal, where He with the others joined them in the evening. Before the supper, the Master set them an example of humility by washing the feet of each. When the meal was over, Our Lord informed them that He knew that one of them would betray Him. Stunned by this news, each one frantically blurted out, "Is it I, Lord?" Judas, sitting near, attempting a pathetic bluff, asked the same question. Our Lord replied quietly, "Thou hast said it." Rejecting the Master's offer of repentance, Judas hurried out into the night.

Then Jesus fulfilled His promise to give His flesh and blood as our food and drink. He blessed and broke bread and giving it to them bade them eat it saying, "This is my body." Then He took the cup and giving thanks gave it to them with the words, "Drink ye all of this. For this is My blood of the New Testament which is shed for many for the remission of sins." In these words Our Lord linked forever the ceremony of the Last Supper with His glorious Sacrifice on Calvary.

Agony in the Garden

AFTER these things, Jesus, as He conversed with them, predicted Peter's denial. He then consoled them in His anxiety for their shock and sorrow over what was now to come. At last they left the supper room and set out for Mount Olivet. Coming to Gethsemane, Jesus led the party to an olive grove. Selecting Peter, James and John, He took them with Him apart from the others. Though desiring their comforting presence, He withdrew to pray alone. Horrified in His human nature at the picture of His coming sufferings, a sickening mixture of sorrow, fright, disgust and frustration flooded His soul. He cried out to His Father for relief, but immediately qualified His prayer with submission, "Thy will be done." Our marriage may bring sufferings demanding like resignation from us.

During this phase an angel appeared to strengthen Him. Yet even with this help, so intense was the agony that blood oozed forth from the pores of His body, and trickled to the ground. Returning to seek solace from them, He found Peter, James and John asleep. Sadly, He chided them, and went back to His prayer and agony. Later, He returned, and again found them asleep. Without a word He went back to face the third and last phase of the agony.

THE AGONY IN THE GARDEN by Heinrich Hofmann

The Arrest, and Peter's Denial

CALM and courageous once more after His agony, Jesus, hearing the approach of those who came to arrest Him, awoke the apostles. He told them that His hour was at hand and intimated that He was going to deliver Himself to them voluntarily. The rabble was made up of some members of the Sanhedrin with their servants and a number of Roman soldiers.

Judas led them towards Jesus, and in utter duplicity greeted Him warmly. Our Lord would have none of his hypocrisy and rebuked him for his betrayal of "the Son of Man with a kiss." Turning from the traitor, He made it clear that He would make their job easy, for He intended to deliver Himself to them. That He gave Himself up to them voluntarily He made even more clear through a miracle. For immediately on His telling them that it was He whom they sought, all the would-be captors nearest Him fell to the ground. Then He allowed them to take Him and they bound Him roughly. Inflamed at this rough handling of the Master he loved, Peter, fiery as ever, took out a sword and slashed at one of His captors, Malchus by name, injuring his right ear. Jesus restrained the apostles, cautioning them against violence, and healed the injured ear. Our Lord was then dragged off, to face the revolting farce that they referred to as a trial.

Meanwhile, what of Peter and the others? After Our Lord's arrest they had fled, but Peter, ashamed of his fear, soon returned and followed a short distance behind Christ's captors. John too came back and joined Peter at Caiaphas' palace. Inside the palace Peter was asked by a portress if he were not one of Christ's disciples. He said in reply, "I am not." Then he joined other servants warming themselves around a fire in the courtyard, where a maid-servant told him that he looked like one of the Twelve. Indignantly he denied it. Still standing by the fire, again he was asked by a servant the same question. This time he denied even knowing Jesus. An hour later some servants told him they were sure he was a follower of Jesus; his very speech gave him away. Peter swore vehemently that he did not know his Master. During these denials the unmistakable crowing of a cock was heard three times. Later, as Our Lord was led from the palace, He fixed on Peter a searching look. His heart crushed, Peter fled from the palace in distraction, and burst into bitter tears.

Peter's defection shows us once more the frailty of human nature. Though Peter loved the Master so much and eventually died for Him, yet now He denied Him. Human love does not erase human weakness, nor do faults mean that love has ceased. Knowing this our marriage will not lead to disillusionment, but rather, well aware of our own faults, we will generously forgive the other as Christ forgave Peter.

PETER'S DENIAL OF JESUS by Carl Bloch

Christ Before Pilate

AT CAIAPHAS' palace the sham continued, with false witnesses adding their quota to the mockery. Jesus, calm and dignified throughout this tournament of falsity, announced quite categorically that He was the Savior, and truly the Son of God. That was all Caiaphas wanted. Calling a halt to the whole pretence, he asked for and obtained from the servile assembly a unanimous vote for the death sentence. Immediately, Our Lord was subjected to revolting treatment by the nonentities who guarded Him. They struck Him, and spat in His face, vying with one another in their cruelty. The gentle, innocent Christ, as the Lamb led to the slaughter, endured all with heroic patience.

Pilate, shallow minded and with little knowledge of the culture of the people he ruled, was, nevertheless, impressed by the dignified bearing of Christ. So he returned Him to the Sanhedrin, and said he saw no reason for their accusations. As he noted the fanatical clamor that his reply set off, Pilate's weakness reasserted itself, and he told them to take Jesus to Herod Antipas, King of Galilee, since the accused was a Galilean, hoping in this way to evade responsibility. Herod simply used this directive as an occasion for clowning and mockery. Jesus was dressed in a white robe, and, in hideous jest, was treated as a fool to entertain the court. Then He was sent back to Pilate.

The Governor, disappointed that he was once more saddled with the responsibility of a decision, told the growing crowd outside his residence that he would punish Christ and release Him, for He did not deserve to die. Strange and distorted justice! Then another thought occurred to him. In deference to Jewish custom, the Romans released a prisoner on the occasion of the paschal festival. So he offered the mob a choice between Barrabbas, a murderer, and Jesus. This, he thought, was the way out. As he awaited the reaction, his wife, Procla, approached and warned him to have nothing to do with "that just man." But the mob's choice was definite and persistent; it wanted Christ crucified. Pilate, thereupon, turned Jesus over to his soldiers to be scourged.

The discussion between Pilate and his wife regarding the problem posed by the mob reminds us of the many problems married life calls on us to face together. The marriage union is so close that the husband and wife cannot have problems that do not affect the other. It is good that these problems be bared and discussed. Too often, unfortunately, husbands and wives decide, as did Pilate, to take the easy way out, to follow the mob, rather than find strength from each other to do what is right.

BEHOLD THE MAN by Bartolomé Esteban Murillo

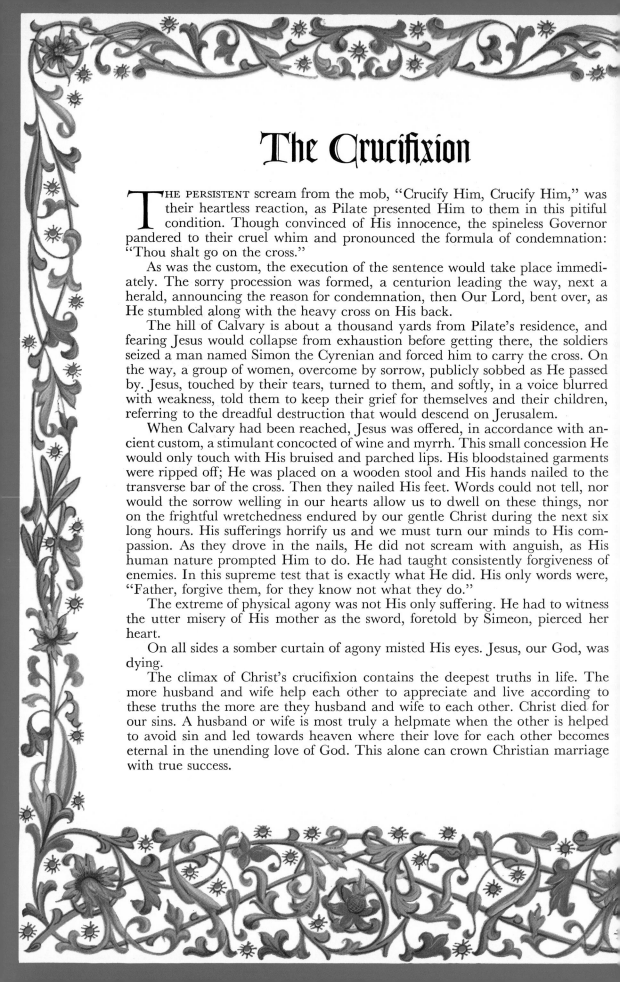

The Crucifixion

THE PERSISTENT scream from the mob, "Crucify Him, Crucify Him," was their heartless reaction, as Pilate presented Him to them in this pitiful condition. Though convinced of His innocence, the spineless Governor pandered to their cruel whim and pronounced the formula of condemnation: "Thou shalt go on the cross."

As was the custom, the execution of the sentence would take place immediately. The sorry procession was formed, a centurion leading the way, next a herald, announcing the reason for condemnation, then Our Lord, bent over, as He stumbled along with the heavy cross on His back.

The hill of Calvary is about a thousand yards from Pilate's residence, and fearing Jesus would collapse from exhaustion before getting there, the soldiers seized a man named Simon the Cyrenian and forced him to carry the cross. On the way, a group of women, overcome by sorrow, publicly sobbed as He passed by. Jesus, touched by their tears, turned to them, and softly, in a voice blurred with weakness, told them to keep their grief for themselves and their children, referring to the dreadful destruction that would descend on Jerusalem.

When Calvary had been reached, Jesus was offered, in accordance with ancient custom, a stimulant concocted of wine and myrrh. This small concession He would only touch with His bruised and parched lips. His bloodstained garments were ripped off; He was placed on a wooden stool and His hands nailed to the transverse bar of the cross. Then they nailed His feet. Words could not tell, nor would the sorrow welling in our hearts allow us to dwell on these things, nor on the frightful wretchedness endured by our gentle Christ during the next six long hours. His sufferings horrify us and we must turn our minds to His compassion. As they drove in the nails, He did not scream with anguish, as His human nature prompted Him to do. He had taught consistently forgiveness of enemies. In this supreme test that is exactly what He did. His only words were, "Father, forgive them, for they know not what they do."

The extreme of physical agony was not His only suffering. He had to witness the utter misery of His mother as the sword, foretold by Simeon, pierced her heart.

On all sides a somber curtain of agony misted His eyes. Jesus, our God, was dying.

The climax of Christ's crucifixion contains the deepest truths in life. The more husband and wife help each other to appreciate and live according to these truths the more are they husband and wife to each other. Christ died for our sins. A husband or wife is most truly a helpmate when the other is helped to avoid sin and led towards heaven where their love for each other becomes eternal in the unending love of God. This alone can crown Christian marriage with true success.

THE CRUCIFIXION by Carl Bloch

Jesus Dies on the Cross

As our savior hung dying on the cross, the soldiers, as was their grisly right according to law, cast lots for His garments, unwittingly fulfilling the prophecy of the twenty-second Psalm which foretells the parting of the Master's garments and the casting of lots on His vesture. The two brigands, crucified on either side of Christ, mingled their mockery with that of the others. They reminded Him of His claim of being able to rebuild the Temple in three days—of His saving others, and contemptuously told Him He now could not save Himself.

Suddenly, however, one of them, realizing the heinousness of it all, turned to Christ, and contritely asked Our Lord to remember him when He shall come as King. The dying Jesus, returning kindness for insult, gently replied, "This day thou shalt be with me in paradise."

Ever a loving Son, Our Lord's thoughts were with His mother. Each pang of grief she suffered He shared with her. Solicitous for her well-being, He committed her to the care of His beloved disciple, John.

As we pause to watch the sufferings of the Savior, we consider the sufferings that are part of life. We remember that in marriage we contracted for the sufferings as well as the joys. We do not know what sufferings lie ahead of us, but we do know that every one's life holds some suffering. Christ's sufferings and death take on a new meaning for us when we recall that they were prompted by love and love alone. From Him alone can we get that kind of love that will prove itself in the face of suffering.

About noon, the heavens marked their disapproval and cast over the dreadful scene a curtain of gloom, which continued till three o'clock. Shortly before that fatal hour, His entire human nature rose in final distress, as cruelty heaped on cruelty, and a cry of utter agony escaped from His lips, "My God, my God, why hast thou forsaken Me?" No words could better portray the extremity of Our Lord's sufferings.

Burning with fever, He gasped, "I thirst," and a bystander took a sponge, dipped in a mixture of vinegar and water, and fastening it to a branch of hyssop held it up to His mouth. His lips thus moistened, He indicated that His work on earth has been accomplished and that He is now ready to die. Quoting the Psalms, He uttered His last words, teeming with love of His Father till the end. "Father into thy hands I commend my spirit." Then with a final cry of pain, His outraged humanity reached the limit of endurance, and Our Savior, Victim for our sins on the altar of the cross, bowed His head and died.

SOLDIERS CASTING LOTS FOR THE GARMENT OF JESUS by James J. J. Tissot

The Resurrection

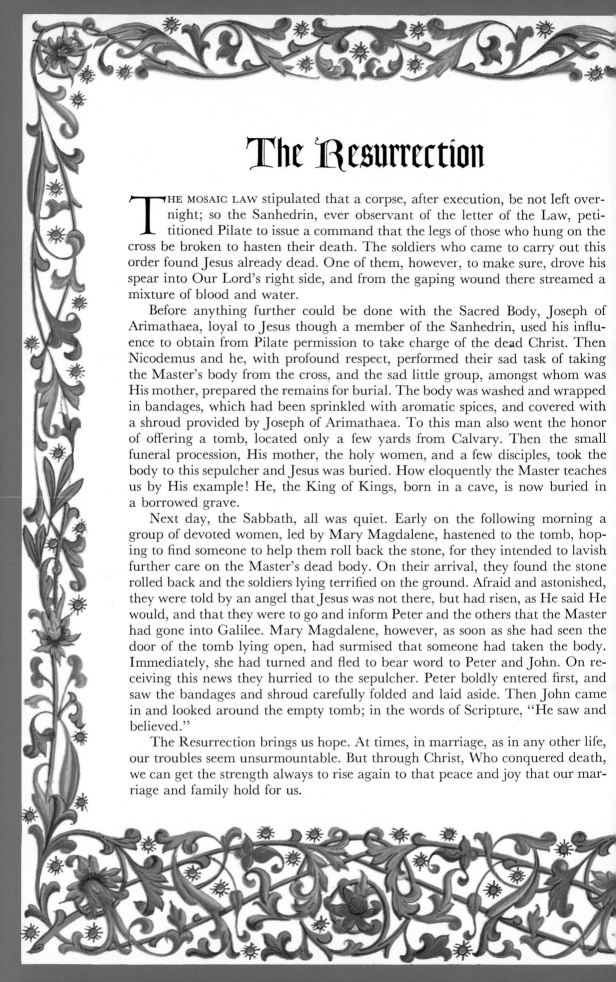

THE MOSAIC LAW stipulated that a corpse, after execution, be not left overnight; so the Sanhedrin, ever observant of the letter of the Law, petitioned Pilate to issue a command that the legs of those who hung on the cross be broken to hasten their death. The soldiers who came to carry out this order found Jesus already dead. One of them, however, to make sure, drove his spear into Our Lord's right side, and from the gaping wound there streamed a mixture of blood and water.

Before anything further could be done with the Sacred Body, Joseph of Arimathaea, loyal to Jesus though a member of the Sanhedrin, used his influence to obtain from Pilate permission to take charge of the dead Christ. Then Nicodemus and he, with profound respect, performed their sad task of taking the Master's body from the cross, and the sad little group, amongst whom was His mother, prepared the remains for burial. The body was washed and wrapped in bandages, which had been sprinkled with aromatic spices, and covered with a shroud provided by Joseph of Arimathaea. To this man also went the honor of offering a tomb, located only a few yards from Calvary. Then the small funeral procession, His mother, the holy women, and a few disciples, took the body to this sepulcher and Jesus was buried. How eloquently the Master teaches us by His example! He, the King of Kings, born in a cave, is now buried in a borrowed grave.

Next day, the Sabbath, all was quiet. Early on the following morning a group of devoted women, led by Mary Magdalene, hastened to the tomb, hoping to find someone to help them roll back the stone, for they intended to lavish further care on the Master's dead body. On their arrival, they found the stone rolled back and the soldiers lying terrified on the ground. Afraid and astonished, they were told by an angel that Jesus was not there, but had risen, as He said He would, and that they were to go and inform Peter and the others that the Master had gone into Galilee. Mary Magdalene, however, as soon as she had seen the door of the tomb lying open, had surmised that someone had taken the body. Immediately, she had turned and fled to bear word to Peter and John. On receiving this news they hurried to the sepulcher. Peter boldly entered first, and saw the bandages and shroud carefully folded and laid aside. Then John came in and looked around the empty tomb; in the words of Scripture, "He saw and believed."

The Resurrection brings us hope. At times, in marriage, as in any other life, our troubles seem unsurmountable. But through Christ, Who conquered death, we can get the strength always to rise again to that peace and joy that our marriage and family hold for us.

THE RESURRECTION by Carl Bloch

The Ascension

SHORTLY after Christ had risen from the dead He appeared to Mary Magdalene. At first she thought He was the gardener and, overcome with grief, pleaded with him to tell her where her dead Master's body had been taken. Then the Savior spoke one word, "Mary." It was enough. Her soul overflowing with faith, love and joy she threw herself at His feet crying out, "Master."

On Sunday afternoon two disciples were on their way from Jerusalem to the village of Emmaus. As they walked along discussing the distressing events of the last few days Jesus joined them. But they did not recognize Him. When they reached Emmaus Jesus accepted their invitation to join them in a meal. Breaking bread, He handed a piece to each. As soon as He had done so the disciples realized that their companion was Jesus; but before they could say a word the Master disappeared.

As the two disciples who had returned from Emmaus and joined the others at Jerusalem excitedly recounted their experience, Jesus joined the group and showed them the wounds in His hands and feet. Eight days later, He returned to rebuke Thomas, absent on the previous occasion, for insisting that he must touch the very wounds before believing that the Master had risen.

Later the apostles left Jerusalem and went to Galilee. One evening, Peter, with six other apostles, set out to fish on the lake. All night they fished, but caught nothing. At dawn, they saw a stranger on the shore, and when they had pulled near, this man told them to cast their net on the other side of the boat. They did so, and immediately made such a catch that they could not raise the net. At once Peter recognized Him, and crying out to the others, "It is the Lord," jumped into the water with his usual impetuosity, and swam the hundred yards to the shore.

In a happy reunion they built a little fire, made a meal at His invitation, and then settled down to hear the Master's words. He took this occasion to continue their training for the commission He had given them to "teach all nations, baptizing them in the name of the Father, and of the Son, and of the Holy Ghost." This training the Holy Spirit would complete on Pentecost.

At the appointed time, Our Lord's devoted followers went to Jerusalem, and were met there by the Master, who imparted to them His final instruction. His last words uttered, Jesus Christ, true God and true man, whose birth was a miracle, left the earth also in miraculous fashion. With His mother, the apostles, disciples, and holy women gathered round Him on Mount Olivet, He bade them farewell, and, as He blessed them, rose in great majesty till a cloud hid Him from sight.

CHRIST ASCENDS INTO HEAVEN by Andreas Herman Hunnaeus

This Portrait

MASTERPIECES of Christian art and a brief narrative have combined their grandeur and simplicity in unfolding this Portrait of Christ. But you alone can add depth to this Portrait, by learning its message and etching its meaning into your marriage.

When that faith and love taught by Christ have saturated your marriage and are the very basis of your family life, you will see the true significance of this Portrait. It is rather like a mirror in which, through constant gazing, husband and wife begin to discern there a likeness that merges them more and more into the likeness of Christ, uniting them more and more to each other as they come closer to Him. As married life goes on, offering the challenges it does, your love for each other, through love of Him, will gain a strength as yet unknown to you. More and more selfishness and pride recede from the picture, yielding place to that love, humility and self-denial so beautifully portrayed for us in the life of the Master. The more your marriage conforms to His teachings, the more shall you see your image and that of your family reflected from the Portrait of Christ.

This, then, is our wish for you on the occasion of your marriage, that, increasingly as the years go on, you will see your own likenesses in this Portrait. We trust that, through meditation on its message, the likeness of Christ will shine through you in all you do, so that you add a personal love for the Person of Christ to the love you have for each other. Then you will have captured the depth as well as the scope and beauty of this Portrait: seeing all things through the eyes of Christ, judging as He would judge, loving as He would love, forgiving as He would forgive.

Such husbands and wives become fathers and mothers endowed with the wisdom and example their children require of them. In such a family true happiness is to be found. For true love binds them together and teaches them that by following in the footsteps of the Master their family will reunite in heaven, when this life's work is over, to dwell with Him there forever.